Preparing FOR Marriage

Help for Christian Couples

JOHN PIPER

Preparing for Marriage: Help for Christian Couples

Revised and Expanded Edition

Copyright © 2018 by Desiring God
Post Office Box 2901
Minneapolis, MN 55402

Published for Desiring God by

CruciformPress

Print/PDF 978-1-941114-58-2
Mobipocket 978-1-941114-59-9
ePub 978-1-941114-60-5

Printed in the United States of America

Unless otherwise indicated,
Scripture quotations are from the ESV Bible
(*The Holy Bible, English Standard* © 2001 by Crossway).
Scripture quotations marked NAS or NASB are taken from the New American Standard Bible® (NASB), Copyright © 1960, 1962, 1963, 1968, 1971, 1972, 1973, 1975, 1977, 1995 by The Lockman Foundation. Used by permission.

All emphases in Scripture quotations have been added by the author.

Contents

Editor's Preface

Getting to know that special someone naturally includes learning about family and friends, education and athletics, favorite pastimes, and your hopes and dreams. Ideally you'll ask each other all kinds of questions, some vital and some trivial, and you'll talk about life's best moments and worst, the brightest places in your background and the darkest.

But what about God? What is his role in your relationship? What do each of you believe about him, and how do you understand his dream for marriage—for your marriage?

At Desiring God, one of our most accessed pages online is a set of questions John Piper put together for couples preparing for marriage (an updated version appears in Appendix I). You'll find many of the typical questions here—about friends and entertainment and lifestyle and children, and many people have found that

John's way of putting these questions helps get right at some pretty deep stuff.

But you'll find other questions here, too—about theology, worship and devotion, and the roles of husband and wife—questions that far too many couples don't think to ask. When preparing for marriage, or even in just beginning to consider it, it can be immensely helpful to have the perspective of someone like John Piper, not only a seasoned husband of nearly 50 years, but also a seasoned pastor, careful thinker, and faithful theologian.

This is a short book. Our vision for it is humble. Our hope is that a few couples—whether dating and considering marriage, or engaged and preparing for marriage—would find some benefit here, getting to know each other better in some of life's most significant matters, and becoming more fit to discern God's leading for their lives.

But John has more to offer than just the pre-marriage questions. We have six short chapters we think you will find helpful together on the road to marriage. Chapter 1 includes John's counsel about engagement, chapter 2 about wedding planning (and finances). Chapter 3 provides invaluable instruction about the beautiful, complementary dynamic the Bible teaches between husband and wife.

Sexual relations in marriage is the topic of chapter 4. (We know some of you may be flipping straight to that one, now that you know it's there. That's okay. Do read the rest of the book when you can!) Here there is so much potential for pleasure, and so much potential for pain. Don't shy away from giving the topic of sex good consideration and honest discussion during your engagement.

Then, in chapter 5, John helps us ponder how we can guard our marriages in a day in which they are under assault from every side. Finally, chapter 6 is based on perhaps John Piper's single most important message on marriage. There he goes more macro than many of us have ever dared to go in thinking about what marriage is, and what God designed it for. This is a glorious, true, life-changing vision.

After John's long list of pre-marriage questions to discuss, the second appendix is about mission together. Marriage is for mission, too. In particular, the focus here is on hospitality. It's a lightly edited sermon from the series that became the book *This Momentary Marriage: A Parable of Permanence*, which is where we'd send you to learn more about marriage following this book. (We'd also want to point you to a 30-day devotional for young married couples called *Happily Ever After: Finding Grace in the Messes of Marriage*, by John Piper and other contributors to desiringGod.org.) For Christians, talking about ministry together, including hospitality (literally, in the New Testament, "love for strangers") is essential preparation.

Marriage is big. What you're considering or preparing for here is no trifle. Don't imagine you can just add marriage as another layer to an already busy life. Marriage demands a full restart. Reevaluate your commitments, check your priorities, rethink your normal. This book and other resources like it can help. It will be well worth your time to ask difficult questions and think hard about the answers. For your joy, the good of others, and the glory of the church's Groom.

David Mathis
Executive Editor
desiringGod.org

1

Don't Waste Your Engagement

This chapter has been adapted from Episode 987 of *Ask Pastor John*, a daily audio program in which John Piper answers tough theological and pastoral questions.

"Pastor John, I'm getting married in exactly 100 days. I'm 21 years old, and my bride-to-be is 18. I'm excited to take on the role of loving a woman like Christ did the church, but as the day draws nearer and nearer I am made more and more aware of my need for wisdom and help to become a husband capable of loving a wife well. I'll be re-listening to all the episodes on marriage. But with all that being said, what advice do you have for me? What are the most important questions we need to ask—and likely are not—due to the rushing excitement of the engagement phase?"

Discuss the Hard Things Now

The more issues you can talk about together before marriage, the better. It is far more frustrating and threatening to think of something after you are married that you should have talked about beforehand. So don't shy away from any issue or conversation with your fiancée because you think this is a good time to try to avoid conflict. Now is the time to have every conflict you *can* have that might come up later. If you think that you can dodge conflicts now so that there will be a more opportune time later, you are mistaken. If you think you *should* avoid conflicts now because a blissful engagement is the path to a blissful marriage, you are badly mistaken. Instead, this is what engagement or courtship is designed for: maximum exposure to what each of you thinks, believes, feels, and does, whether habitually or occasionally. No secrets, nothing held back. You don't want marriage to be based on ignorance, but on trust, in the face of all truth.

> *While the topics covered in the six chapters of this book could prompt hours of fruitful conversation (and possibly some constructive conflict along the way), don't miss Appendix 1, either. There you will find more than fifty short, specific questions, in eleven categories, that many couples have found helpful.*

Spiritual Leadership

The next thing I would say is that these are golden months in which to set patterns of spiritual leadership. Take the initiative to read the Bible with your bride-to-be, to pray and think and study and talk together with her about all kinds of biblical and spiritual realities. Make sure the two of you are sufficiently on the same theological page. That is not an artificial or secondary expectation. If the two of you are going to pull together shoulder-to-shoulder in marriage for some great purpose—which is what marriage is for—you must be pulling in the same direction. That is, you must be seeing God in the same way and seeing Christ and seeing the Holy Spirit and seeing faith and seeing love and salvation and heaven and hell and Satan and sin and holiness and obedience—seeing all these things in essentially the same way. Otherwise, pulling together in harness will start to become very painful as you jerk each other around in different directions spiritually. What's more likely, though, is something even worse: that in your marriage you gradually just stop talking about spiritual things. So take the initiative and go deep into every dimension of spiritual life that you can in these days.

Individual Godward Fellowship

And for both of you, you must be aware that your own personal fellowship of faith and joy and hope and obedience toward Jesus is foundational for the survival and flourishing of your marriage. The marriages that I have seen unravel, unravel in tandem with the unraveling of spiritual reality. One or both of the members of these couples falls away from Jesus to one degree or another. When that happens, their spiritual resources for handling normal, everyday conflicts start to evaporate.

Don't just think that what you do *together* strengthens

the marriage. Far more important—and this may sound like an overstatement, but I've thought about it and I am going to stick by it—far more important is what you do *apart* from each other as each of you meets Jesus and consecrates yourself afresh, over and over, so that your devotion to Christ is absolutely unshakable, and your experience of him is profoundly satisfying. I mean separately, personally, as individuals before Christ. When two people operate out of that individual profundity, the marriage will endure. And not only endure, but flourish with joy and fruitfulness.

Expressions of Love and Care

Finally, of all the hundreds of things that need to be said and could be said, here is one last thing that must be said—to both of you, but with special emphasis to you as the man in this relationship: don't assume that your affection for your bride-to-be is known and felt by her. Instead, put it on your lips over and over again, every day. Commit to doing that, from today until the end of your life together. Find fresh ways to say it—not just show it, but say it.

Lots of married men think, *Well, I show it. I earn a living. I guard her. I protect her...* Yes, that's all well and good. Show it. Do the kinds of deeds she loves for you to do. But don't just do things. Say things. Lavish her (and in some different ways when you're married!) with expressions of delight and appreciation and admiration and affection and enjoyment. In your wedding vows, I hope you are going to promise to cherish her above all others and forsake everyone else, cleaving to her alone. Put that cherishing and that cleaving into words every day. This will pay dividends of great joy and deep bonding of soul at a wonderfully profound and happy level.

That said, one caveat: remember that there is a warning in the Bible not to stir up love until it satisfies (see Song 2:7). I think that means, among other things, you can immerse yourself in the Song of Solomon in a premature and inappropriate way, because the language can turn you on in premature ways. But—I am going to risk it anyway and say this—go to that book and learn what I am talking about here. Learn how to put into words, to her face, the cherishing that you feel for her. May God bless you in this season of engagement.

2
Weddings: Don't Break the Bank

This chapter has been adapted from Episode 875 of *Ask Pastor John.*

"Dear Pastor John, in a recent article, you wrote: 'Pastors should lead the way in cultivating a church ethos where expensive funerals (and weddings!) are not the norm.' This is something I hadn't given much thought to before, and really appreciated. Thank you! I was hoping you could speak more directly on the topic of expensive weddings. How can we design a 'Christ-exalting, simple wedding'?"

Word to Pastors

I will make a plea to couples in a minute for courage to be counter-cultural in this regard—because that is what it's going to take—but in that article I am mainly pleading with pastors. I want to see pastors take the initiative to teach and preach and help to build a culture of simplicity in the church that makes the focus of marriage celebrations the Lord Jesus; the Christ-exalting meaning of marriage; the awesome importance of the vows; and the preciousness of the people, the lovers—*not* the clothing, the flowers, the location, the music, and the whole production that can make the actual act of God in marriage seem like an incidental prelude to the big, fancy party afterwards. That is sad, I think.

But, of course, this is not an attack on joy. Just the opposite. It is a plea for drinking from the deepest pools of joy, not the peripheral puddles of happiness. Godly poor people regularly have more joy than rich people. There is no correlation between expensive and joyful—none. Unless it is this: more expensive means more hassle, more stress, more distraction—less joyful. This is a plea to leaders to cultivate an expectation of simplicity so that no one with modest means—and that is a lot of people—feels as though a simple wedding with a mints-and-nuts reception—no meal, no dance, just joy—is somehow less honoring to the Lord and the couple. It is tragic if we have cultivated a situation like that.

Revolution in Resources

Here is the underlying worldview. A decisive turn happened in redemptive history when Jesus came into the world. The Old Testament was, by and large, a come-and-see religion, while the New Testament is largely a go-and-tell religion. That is why there is lavish expenditure in the Old Testament on the temple. *Come see, from Egypt and from Ethiopia and from the ends of the earth! Come see this expensive temple that we have built!* That's why wealth was seen so regularly as a sign of God's blessing. But that has all radically changed with the coming of the Son of Man, who had no place to lay his head and told us to go risk our lives to disciple the nations (see Matthew 8:20; 28:19). We are not living in Old Testament times. This is not a come-and-see religion, and Christianity doesn't even have a geographic center. This is a go-and-tell religion.

The coming of the new covenant has brought a revolution in the use of our resources. What governs our lifestyle now is the effort to show that our treasure is in heaven and not on the earth. What governs us is the effort to maximize our giving to finish the Great Commission and to love the hurting of the world. The New Testament is relentless in pushing us toward simplicity and economy for the kingdom and away from luxury and away from affluence and away from finery, including luxurious weddings.

Just to give you a taste of what I mean when I say it is relentless, consider a few Bible verses.

- Blessed are you who are poor, for yours is the kingdom of God... Woe to you who are rich, for you have received your consolation. (Luke 6:20, 24)
- They are choked by the cares and riches and pleasures of life. (Luke 8:14)
- The Son of Man has nowhere to lay his head. (Luke 9:58)
- Do not lay up for yourselves treasures on earth, where moth and rust destroy. (Matthew 6:19)
- I tell you, do not be anxious about your life... Life [is] more than food... and clothing. (Matthew 6:25)

- Sell your possessions, and give to the needy. Provide yourselves with…a treasure in the heavens. (Luke 12:33)
- Any one of you who does not renounce all that he has cannot be my disciple. (Luke 14:33)
- How difficult it is for those who have wealth to enter the kingdom of God! (Luke 18:24)
- Paul was "poor, yet making many rich." He had "nothing, yet [possessed] everything." (2 Corinthians 6:10)
- We brought nothing into the world, and we cannot take anything out of the world. But if we have food and clothing, with these we will be content. (1 Timothy 6:7–8)
- You joyfully accepted the plundering of your property, since you knew that you yourselves had a better possession and an abiding one. (Hebrews 10:34)

When Noël and I were married, she wore her mother's wedding dress. There were some small alterations made, but the cost was minimal. I wore my best and only Sunday suit, and my best man wore his. Noël's matron of honor wore a nice Sunday dress. We had an open Bible and a cross on the platform, just to show our values. Someone played the church organ. My father preached. The church provided a reception in the fellowship hall: no meal, no refreshments, just a cake. For the honeymoon, I borrowed my father's car and we made the seven-hour drive to St. Petersburg, Florida, where we stayed in a single-story motel on the beach.

It was all simple. It was all full of joy. It was explosive with happy expectation. Nobody borrowed any money.

The Lord, the word of God, the vows, and the lovers were in the foreground, and God was honored. And all these decades later we are just as married as anybody. I think that is a good idea.

Truth and Beauty, in Humility

Now, let me stress again that there *is* a place for special: special dress, special expenditures, special beauty in the simplicity of the Christian life. There *is* a place for beauty expressed in that way. But what is happening in the evangelical church today, it seems to me, is that things are careening out of control, and somebody needs to put the brakes on. So I am pleading with pastors, especially. Let the service and the word and the vows and the Lord and the love be the main thing. There does not have to be a meal after the wedding—believe me, there doesn't. There doesn't have to be a dance. The reception doesn't have to be at an expensive hotel. There doesn't have to be a paid quintet. Really, it doesn't have to be.

Besides pastors who lead on this, the church needs young people with backbone and radical Christian courage to stand against a culture and show in all humility what truth and beauty and joy can look like at one fourth the cost and one fourth the anxieties and one fourth the stress—and double the focus on the glory of Christ and the advancement of his kingdom. I pray that you two might be among them.

EPHESIANS 5:21-33

[Submit] to one another out of reverence for Christ. [22] Wives, submit to your own husbands, as to the Lord. [23] For the husband is the head of the wife even as Christ is the head of the church, his body, and is himself its Savior. [24] Now as the church submits to Christ, so also wives should submit in everything to their husbands. [25] Husbands, love your wives, as Christ loved the church and gave himself up for her, [26] that he might sanctify her, having cleansed her by the washing of water with the word, [27] so that he might present the church to himself in splendor, without spot or wrinkle or any such thing, that she might be holy and without blemish. [28] In the same way husbands should love their wives as their own bodies. He who loves his wife loves himself. [29] For no one ever hated his own flesh, but nourishes and cherishes it, just as Christ does the church, [30] because we are members of his body. [31] "Therefore a man shall leave his father and mother and hold fast to his wife, and the two shall become one flesh." [32] This mystery is profound, and I am saying that it refers to Christ and the church. [33] However, let each one of you love his wife as himself, and let the wife see that she respects her husband.

1 PETER 3:1-7

Likewise, wives, be subject to your own husbands, so that even if some do not obey the word, they may be won without a word by the conduct of their wives, [2] when they see your respectful and pure conduct. [3] Do not let your adorning be external— the braiding of hair and the putting on of gold jewelry, or the clothing you wear—[4] but let your adorning be the hidden person of the heart with the imperishable beauty of a gentle and quiet spirit, which in God's sight is very precious. [5] For this is how the holy women who hoped in God used to adorn themselves, by submitting to their own husbands, [6] as Sarah obeyed Abraham, calling him lord. And you are her children, if you do good and do not fear anything that is frightening. [7] Likewise, husbands, live with your wives in an understanding way, showing honor to the woman as the weaker vessel, since they are heirs with you of the grace of life, so that your prayers may not be hindered.

3

Husbands Who Love Like Christ and the Wives Who Submit to Them

The sections of Ephesians and 1 Peter on the preceding page are essential passages for engaged or newly married Christian couples to become familiar with and to discuss, honestly and in detail. My goal in this chapter is to encourage that conversation by giving you plenty to talk about.

Let's start by jumping into the Ephesians passage at verse 31. It's a quote from Genesis 2:24, "Therefore a man shall leave his father and his mother and hold fast to his wife, and they shall become one flesh." In the next verse, Paul looks back on this quote and says, "This mystery is profound, and I am saying that it refers to Christ and the church."

Mystery of Marriage

Why is the coming together of a man and woman to form one flesh in marriage a mystery? Paul's answer is this: the marriage union is a mystery because its deepest meaning has been partially concealed, but is now being openly revealed by the apostle: "it refers to Christ and the church" (v. 32).

So marriage is like a metaphor or an image or a picture or a parable that stands for something *more* than a man and a woman becoming one flesh. It stands for the relationship between Christ and the church. That's the deepest meaning of marriage. It's meant to be a living drama of how Christ and the church relate to each other.

Notice how verses 28–30 describe the parallel between Christ and the church being one body, and the husband and wife being one flesh. "In the same way husbands should love their wives as their own bodies. He who loves his wife loves himself. For no one ever hated his own flesh, but nourishes and cherishes it, just as Christ does the church, because we are members of his body." In other words, the one-flesh union between man and wife means that in a sense they are now one body, so that the care a husband has for his wife, he has for himself. They are one. What he does to her, he does to himself. Then Paul compares this to Christ's care for the church. Picking up near the end of verse 29, he says the husband nourishes and cherishes his own flesh, "as Christ does the church, because we are members of his body."

Just as the husband is one flesh with his wife, so the church is one body with Christ. When the husband cherishes and nourishes his wife, he cherishes and nourishes himself; and when Christ cherishes and nourishes the church, he cherishes and nourishes himself.

If you want to understand God's meaning for marriage, you have to grasp that we are dealing with an original and a copy; a reality and a metaphor; a truth and a parable. The *original*—the reality, the truth—is God's marriage to his people, or Christ's marriage to the church. And the *copy*—the metaphor, the parable—is a husband's marriage to his wife. Geoffrey Bromiley says, "As God made man in his own image, so he made earthly marriage in the image of his own eternal marriage with his people" (*God and Marriage*, p. 43).

Roles of Husbands and Wives

One thing to learn from this mystery is the roles of husband and wife in marriage. One of Paul's points in this passage is that these roles are not arbitrarily assigned, and they are not reversible without obscuring God's purpose for marriage. The roles of husband and wife are rooted in the distinctive roles of Christ and his church. God means for marriage to say something, about his Son and his church, in the way husbands and wives relate to each other.

We see this in verses 23–25. Verse 24 speaks to the wife about her half of the metaphor, and verses 23 and 25 speak about the husband's half of the metaphor. Wives, find your distinctive role as a wife in keying off the way the church relates to Christ. "Now as the church submits to Christ, so also wives should submit in everything to their husbands" (v. 24). Then to husbands: find your distinctive role as a husband in keying off the way Christ relates to the church. "For the husband is the head of the wife even as Christ is the head of the church, his body, and is himself its Savior" (v. 23). "Husbands, love your wives, as Christ loved the church and gave himself up for her" (v. 25).

I need to be a humble servant to my wife just as Christ gave himself up for the church.

Redeeming of Headship and Submission

When sin entered the world, it ruined the harmony of marriage (see Genesis 1–3). Not because it brought headship and submission into existence, but because it twisted man's humble, loving headship into hostile domination in some men, and into lazy indifference in others. And it twisted woman's intelligent, willing submission into manipulative obsequiousness in some women, and into brazen insubordination in others. Sin didn't *create* headship and submission; it distorted them and inclined them toward being ugly and destructive. Now if this is true, then the redemption we anticipate with the coming of Christ is not the *dismantling* of the original, created order of loving headship and willing submission, but a recovery of it from the ravages of sin. And that's just what we find in Ephesians 5:21–33. Wives, let your fallen submission be redeemed by modeling it after God's intention for the church! Husbands, let your fallen headship be redeemed by modeling it after God's intention for Christ!

Therefore, headship is not a man's right to command and control. It's a responsibility to love like Christ; to lay down your life for your wife in servant-leadership. And submission is not slavish or coerced or cowering. That's not the way Christ wants the church to respond to his leadership: he wants it to be free and willing and glad and refining and strengthening.

So this passage of Scripture does two things: it guards against the abuses of headship by telling husbands to love like Jesus; and it guards against the debasing of submission by telling wives to respond the way the church does to Christ.

Defining Headship and Submission

It may be helpful here to offer crisp definitions of headship and submission as I understand them from this text.

- *Headship* is the divine calling of a husband to take primary responsibility for Christlike servant-leadership, protection, and provision in the home.
- *Submission* is the divine calling of a wife to honor and affirm her husband's leadership, and help carry it through according to her gifts.

I'll offer some practical implications of these definitions in a moment. But first let me say a word about a couple of common objections.

What about Mutual Submission?

The ideas of headship and submission are not popular today. The spirit of our society makes it very hard for people to even hear texts like this in a positive way. The most common objection to the picture I just painted of loving leadership and willing submission is that verse 21 teaches us to be mutually submissive to each other, "submitting to one another out of reverence for Christ."

So one writer says, "By definition, mutual submission rules out hierarchical differences" (Gilbert Bilezikian, *Beyond Sex Roles*, p. 154). He is claiming here that if mutual submission is a reality between husband and wife, then it's a contradiction to say the husband has a special responsibility to lead and the wife a special responsibility to support that leadership and help carry it through.

What shall we say to this? I will say that it is simply not true. In fact, the writer himself says one page later that, "The church thrives on mutual subjection. In a Spirit-led church, the elders submit to the congregation in being accountable for their watch-care, and the congregation submits to the elders in accepting their guidance" (p. 155). Later he even says, "The congregations submit to their leaders by obeying" (p. 251). So we see that, when it comes to the church, he has no trouble acknowledging how mutual submission is possible between two groups, one of which has the special responsibility to guide, and the other of which has the special responsibility to accept guidance.

And that's right. There is no contradiction between mutual submission and a relationship of leadership and response. Mutual submission doesn't mean that both partners must submit in exactly the same ways. Christ submitted himself to the church in one way, by a kind of servant-leadership that cost him his life. And the church submits herself to Christ in another way by honoring his leadership and following him on the Calvary road.

So it is not true that mutual submission rules out the family pattern of Christlike leadership and church-like submission. Mutual submission doesn't obliterate those roles; it transforms them!

Does *Head* Even Refer to Leadership?

One other common objection to the pattern of leadership and submission is that *head* does not mean "leadership" at all. It means "source," like a fountainhead or the head of a river (Bilezikian, pp. 157–162). By this view, to call a husband the "head" of his wife wouldn't mean he is to be a leader, but in some sense is her "source" or "fountainhead."

In fact, however, there are serious studies showing that this was not a normal meaning for the word *head* in Paul's day. But you'll probably never read these technical articles, so let me try to show you something from the verses themselves that everyone can see.

The husband is pictured as the head of his wife, just as Christ is pictured as the head of the church, his body (see Ephesians 5:23). Now if *head* means "source," then what is the husband the source of? What does the body get from the head? It gets nourishment (that's mentioned in verse 29). And we can understand that, because the mouth is in the head, and nourishment comes through the mouth to the body. But that's not all the body gets from the head. It gets guidance because the eyes are in the head. And it gets alertness and protection because the ears are in the head.

Thus, if the husband as "head" is one flesh with his wife, his body, and if he is therefore her source of guidance and food and alertness, then the natural conclusion is that the head, the husband, has a primary responsibility for leadership and provision and protection. So even if you take *head* to mean "source," the most natural interpretation of these verses is that husbands are called by God to take primary responsibility for Christlike servant-leadership and protection and provision in the home. And wives are called to honor and affirm the husband's leadership and help carry it through according to her gifts.

Practical Implications

In closing out this chapter, we will now briefly examine some practical implications of this view.

Transformation of Leading

The call in verse 25 for husbands to, "Love your wives, as Christ loved the church and gave himself up for her," revolutionizes the way he leads. Notice in Luke 22:26 where Jesus says, "Let the greatest among you become as the youngest, and the leader as one who serves." In other words: husbands, don't stop leading, but turn all your leading into serving. The responsibility of leadership is given not to puff yourself up, but to build your family up.

Transformation of Submission

Submission does not mean putting the husband in the place of Christ. Verse 21 says that submission comes out of reverence *for* Christ. Submission does not mean that the husband's word is absolute, for only Christ's word is absolute. No wife should follow a husband into sin; you can't do that "out of reverence for Christ."

And submission does not mean surrendering thought. It does not mean a wife having no input on family decisions or no influence on her husband—because submission does not come from ignorance or incompetence. It comes from what is fitting and appropriate in God's created order (see Colossians 3:18). Submission is an inclination of the will to say *yes* to the husband's leadership, and a disposition of the spirit to support his initiatives. The reason I say it's a disposition and an inclination is because there will be times when the most submissive wife will hesitate at a husband's decision. It may look unwise to her.

Suppose it's Noël and me. I am about to decide something foolish for the family. At that moment, Noël could express her submission something like this, "Johnny,

I know you've thought a lot about this, and I love it when you take the initiative to plan for us and take the responsibility like this, but I really don't have peace about this decision and I think we need to talk about it some more. Could we? Maybe tonight sometime?"

The reason that is a biblical form of submission is because:

1. Husbands, unlike Christ, are fallible and ought to admit it;
2. Husbands ought to want their wives to be excited about the family decisions, because Christ wants us to be excited about following his decisions and not just follow begrudgingly;
3. The way Noël expressed her misgivings communicated clearly that she endorses my leadership and affirms me in my role as head.

When a man senses a primary, God-given responsibility for the spiritual life of the family—gathering the family for devotions, taking them to church, calling for prayer at meals—when he senses a primary, God-given responsibility for the discipline and education of the children, the stewardship of money, the provision of food, the safety of the home, the healing of discord—that special sense of responsibility is not authoritarian or autocratic or domineering or bossy or oppressive or abusive. It is simply servant-leadership. And I have never met a wife who is sorry she is married to a man like that. Because when God designs a thing (like marriage), he designs it for his glory and our good.

So again, let get me encourage you and your fiancé(e) to review this chapter carefully. What sections cause your

heart to soar? Does anything here make you apprehen-
sive or uneasy? Are there passages that trouble you—not
because you don't like the way I've expressed something,
but because you find yourself resisting the teaching of
Scripture? Let your sharing and conversation be free and
open and honest. Grappling with Scripture is never a bad
idea. Be kind and humble, and God will do a good work in
you both.

HEBREWS 13:4-5

Let marriage be held in honor among all, and let the marriage bed be undefiled, for God will judge the sexually immoral and adulterous. [5] Keep your life free from love of money, and be content with what you have, for he has said, "I will never leave you nor forsake you."

4
Sexual Relations in Marriage

It is interesting that Hebrews puts money and the marriage bed side-by-side. That's no coincidence. In fact, most counselors today would put money and sexual relations near the top of their list of trouble spots in marriage. And while our focus in this chapter is on verse 4 (sexual relations in marriage), we will soon see—perhaps unexpectedly—that verse 5 (money, desire, contentment, and God's provision) is equally pertinent.

Faith, Sin, and Contentment

"Let marriage be held in honor among all, and let the marriage bed be undefiled." That is, let sexual relations in marriage be kept pure, clean, free from blemish. All these terms are simply visual or tangible metaphors for a moral demand—don't sin in your sexual relations in marriage. But what is sin? Essentially, sin is any act or attitude that displeases God. And I find it very helpful to focus on the essential nature of sin as it relates to the great positive force in the Christian life: faith.

Hebrews 11:6 says, "Without faith it is impossible to please [God]." Adding this verse to our consideration leads us to two points.

1. Because sin is anything that displeases God, and without faith you *can't* please God, then if you don't have faith, everything you do is sin, because everything you do displeases God.
2. This suggests strongly that there must be a close, perhaps causal, connection between sin and the *absence* of faith. And Romans 14:23 confirms such a connection, telling us, "Whatever does not proceed from faith is sin."

In other words, the essential nature of those actions and attitudes we call sin is that they are not prompted or motivated by a heart of faith. The thing that makes an attitude or act displeasing to God is that it does not grow from faith in God. Sin is evil precisely in its failure to be a product of faith.

At this point, we need to clarify how it is that our actions come either "from faith" or not from faith. First of all, what is this faith that produces attitudes and actions which aren't sin? Hebrews 11:1 says, "Faith is the assurance of things hoped for, the conviction of things not seen." Faith, therefore, is the confidence we feel in the good things that God has promised to do for us, tomorrow and to eternity. We can't see them, but faith is the assurance that the promises in which we hope will come true. Hebrews 11:6 in its entirety says, "Without faith it is impossible to please him, for whoever would draw near to God must believe that he exists and that he rewards those who seek him." So the faith that pleases God is this: our coming to him with confidence that, perhaps contrary to all appearances, he will reward us with all the good things he has promised.

Now, how does such faith produce attitudes and acts which are not sin? Hebrews 13:5 says, "Keep your life free from love of money, and be content with what you have." The love of money is a desire that displeases God; it is sin. And 1 Timothy 6:10 says, "The love of money is a root of all kinds of evils." Now the antidote to this sinful love and all the evils that grow from it is *contentment*: "Be content with what you have." But the writer doesn't leave us there, by ourselves, to somehow crank up contentment. He goes on to give a basis for our contentment: "For [God] has said, 'I will never leave you nor forsake you.'"

The basis for contentment is the promise of God's unfailing help and fellowship. That promise is taken from Deuteronomy 31:6, "Be strong and courageous. Do not fear or be in dread of them, for it is the LORD your God who goes with you. He will not leave you or forsake you."

So the writer to the Hebrews is saying this: *God has made such comforting, reassuring, hope-inspiring promises in his word that, if we have faith in these promises, we will be content, and that contentment is the antidote to the love of money, which is the root of all sorts of evils.*

Now we can see more clearly how it is that an action or attitude comes "from faith" or not. If we do not have faith—if we do not trust the promise of God that says, "I will never leave you nor forsake you"—then we will feel anxious and insecure, and the deceptive power of money to buy the sense of security and peace we lack will be so attractive that it will start to produce other evils in us. We will be inclined to steal, or lie on our income tax returns, or rationalize why we shouldn't be giving generously to the church, or conveniently forget about a debt we owe a friend, or refuse to spend any money to make our rental property more livable, and on and on. The evils that come from the love of money are endless. And the reason these evils are sin is that they do not come from faith.

If we have faith in the promise, "I will never leave you nor forsake you," then we will be free from the anxiety and insecurity that craves more money, and we will have victory over the sins that result from the love of money. If you are content in Christ, resting in the promise of God always to help you and stay beside you, then the compulsion to steal and lie on your tax return, and skimp on your giving, and neglect your debts, and oppress poor renters will be gone. Instead there will be an honest day's work, complete accuracy on the tax return, generosity to the church, faithfulness in retiring debts, and doing unto your renters as you would have them do to you. And all this new behavior will not be sin but righteousness, because it comes from faith in the hope-giving promise of God.

Just in case you have lost the connection between all this and sexual relations in marriage, let's go back and pick up the thread. Hebrews 13:4 says, "Let marriage be held in honor among all, and let the marriage bed be undefiled." That means to let the marriage bed be without sin; to not sin in your sexual relations. Now we have seen that sin is whatever is not from faith. Sin is what you feel and think and do when you are not taking God at his word and resting in his promises. So the command of Hebrews

13:4 can be stated like this: *Let your sexual relations be free from any act or attitude that does not come from faith in God's Word.* Or to put it positively: *have* those attitudes and *do* those acts in your marital sexual relations which grow out of the contentment that comes from confidence in God's promises.

Why Seek Sexual Gratification in Marriage?

But now immediately a problem emerges. Someone may ask, "If I am content through faith in God's promises, why should I even seek sexual gratification at all?" That is a good question. And the first answer to it is, "Maybe you shouldn't seek any sexual gratification; maybe you should stay single." This is what Paul was urging in 1 Corinthians 7:6–7. He says, in effect, "By no means am I commanding everyone to get married and gratify sexual desires. All I'm saying is that sexual desire is okay, and if a person has a compelling desire, marriage is the place to satisfy it." But he also added, "I wish that all were [single] as I myself am. But each has his own special gift from God, one of one kind and one of another" (v. 7).

This really is a remarkable verse. Paul could wish that everyone were single like him—free from the entanglements of family life and from the strong urge to be married. But he knows that's not God's will, for "Each has his own gift from God." God wills some people to be married and some to be single. He does not gift everyone like Paul; some he gifts like Peter, who took his wife with him on his missionary travels (see 1 Corinthians 9:5). So the first answer to the question, "If I have contentment through faith in God's promises, why should I seek sexual gratification?" is, "Perhaps you shouldn't. God may want you single."

But there is a second answer to this question, and it relates to the fact that the contentment God promises to give does not mean the end of all desires, especially bodily desires. Even Jesus, whose faith was perfect, got hungry and desired food, and got tired and desired rest. Sexual appetite is in this same category. The contentment of faith does not take it away any more than it takes away hunger and weariness. What, then, does contentment mean in relation to ongoing sexual desire? I think it means two things.

1. If gratification of that desire is denied through singleness, then that denial will be compensated for by an abundant portion of God's help and fellowship through faith. In Philippians 4:11–13 Paul said, "Not that I am speaking of being in need, for I have learned in whatever situation I am to be content…I have learned the secret of facing plenty and hunger, abundance and need. I can do all things through him who strengthens me." If Paul could learn to be content in hunger, then we can learn to be content if God chooses not to give us sexual gratification.

2. The other thing contentment means in relation to ongoing sexual desire is this: if gratification is not denied us but offered to us in marriage, we will seek it and enjoy it only in ways that reflect our faith. To put it another way, while the contentment of faith does not put an end to our hunger, weariness, or sexual appetite, it does transform the way we go about satis-

fying those desires. Faith doesn't stop us from eating, but it stops gluttony. It doesn't stop sleep, but it keeps us from being a sluggard. It doesn't stop sexual appetite but… But what? That's what we want to spend the rest of this chapter trying to answer, though space here only allows a very partial answer.

Because Faith Believes That Sex Is a Good Gift of God

First of all, when the ear of faith hears the word from 1 Timothy 4:4–5 that, "Everything created by God is good, and nothing is to be rejected if it is received with thanksgiving, for it is made holy by the word of God and prayer"—when the ear of faith hears that, it believes. And so faith honors the body and its appetites as God's good gifts. Faith will not allow a married couple to lie in bed and say to themselves, "What we are doing is dirty; it's what they do in the pornographic movies." Instead, faith says, "God created this act, and it is good, and it is for 'those who believe and know the truth'" (1 Timothy 4:3). It is the world that has plundered God's gifts and corrupted them by misuse. But these gifts belong rightfully to the children of God, and so faith will not let us view them as worldly or defiled. "Let marriage be held in *honor* among all, and let the marriage bed be undefiled."

Because Faith Frees from the Guilt of the Past

Secondly, faith increases the joy of sexual relations in marriage because it frees from the guilt of the past. I have in view, mainly, we who are married but have to look back on an act of fornication, or adultery, or incest, or a homosexual fling, or years of habitual masturbation, or preoccupation with pornography, or promiscuous petting, or divorce. And what I have to say to us is this: if it genuinely lies within you, by the grace of God, to throw yourself on the mercy of God for forgiveness, then he will free you from the guilt of the past.

- There is therefore now no condemnation for those who are in Christ Jesus. (Romans 8:1)
- To the one who does not work but believes in him who justifies the ungodly, his faith is counted as righteousness. (Romans 4:5)
- Blessed is the one whose transgression is forgiven, whose sin is covered. Blessed is the man against whom the LORD counts no iniquity. (Psalm 32:1–2)
- He does not deal with us according to our sins, nor repay us according to our iniquities. For as high as the heavens are above the earth, so great is his steadfast love toward those who fear him; as far as the east is from the west, so far does he remove our transgressions from us. (Psalm 103:10–12)
- If we confess our sins, he is faithful and just to forgive us our sins and to cleanse us from all unrighteousness. (1 John 1:9)

There is no need for a child of God to carry any guilt into the marriage bed. But that takes a solid faith because Satan loves to make us feel unforgiven for the rottenness of our former life.

"Resist him, firm in your faith" (1 Peter 5:9). Quench his flaming darts with the shield of faith (see Ephesians 6:16); faith in "the Son of God, who loved [you] and gave

himself for [you]" (Galatians 2:20); who for your sake was
made to be sin that you might become the righteousness of God (see 2 Corinthians 5:21); who "bore [your]
sins in his body on the tree" (1 Peter 2:24). Lay hold on
your forgiveness, and take it with you to the marriage bed.
Christ died for your sin, that in him you might have guilt-
free sexual relations in marriage.

Of course, this is not always easy. Even though the
guilt of our sin can be washed away, some of the scars
remain. I can imagine a couple just before their engagement sitting together in a park. He turns to her and says,
"There is something that I've got to say. Two years ago I
had sexual relations with another girl. I was away from the
Lord, and it was just one night. I've wept over that one
night many times. I believe God has forgiven me and I
hope you can." In the weeks that follow, not without tears,
she forgives him, and they marry. And on their first honeymoon night they lie together, and as he looks at her, the
tears well up in her eyes and he says, "What's the matter?"
And she says, "I just can't help but think of that other girl,
that she lay right here where I am." And years later, when
the novelty of his wife's body has worn off, he finds himself
inadvertently drifting back in his imagination to the thrill
of that one-night fling. That's what I mean by scars. And
all of us have such scars. All of us have committed sins
which, though forgiven, make our present life more prob-
lematic than if we hadn't committed them.

But I do not want to give the impression that Christ
is powerless against such scars. He may not remove all the
problems that these scars cause us, but he has promised to
work for our good, even in all these problems, if we love
him and are called according to his purpose.

Take the imaginary couple I just referred to. I prefer to think that there was a happy ending. That they came eventually to a satisfying sexual relationship because they worked at it openly in constant prayer and reliance on the grace of God. They talked about all their feelings. They kept nothing bottled up. They trusted each other and helped each other, and they found their way to peace and sexual harmony and, above all, new dimensions of God's grace.

Christ died not only that in him we might have guilt-free sexual relations in marriage, but also that he might then, even through our scars, convey to us some spiritual good.

Because Faith Uses Sex as a Weapon against Satan

The third thing that we can say about faith and sexual relations in marriage is that faith uses sex against Satan. Look at 1 Corinthians 7:3–5.

> The husband should give to his wife her conjugal rights, and likewise the wife to her husband. [4] For the wife does not have authority over her own body, but the husband does. Likewise the husband does not have authority over his own body, but the wife does. [5] Do not deprive one another, except perhaps by agreement for a limited time, that you may devote yourselves to prayer; but then come together again, so that Satan may not tempt you because of your lack of self-control.

In Ephesians 6:16, Paul says we should ward off Satan with the shield of faith. Here he essentially says to married people, "Ward off Satan with sufficient sexual intercourse. Don't abstain too long, but come together soon, so that Satan will gain no foothold." Well, which is it? Do we guard ourselves from Satan with the shield of faith or the shield of sex?

The answer for married people is that *faith makes use of sexual intercourse as a means of grace.* For the people whom God leads into marriage, sexual relations are a God-ordained means of overcoming temptation to sin (the sin of adultery, the sin of sexual fantasizing, the sin of pornographic reading, etc.). Faith humbly accepts such gifts and offers thanks.

Now notice something else in that 1 Corinthians passage quoted above. Paul says that the man and the woman have rights over each other's body. When the two become one flesh, their bodies are at each other's disposal. Each has the right to lay claim to the other's body for sexual gratification. But what we really need to see is what Paul commands in verses 3 and 5 in view of these mutual rights. He does not say, "Therefore stake your claim! Take your rights!" He says, "Husband, give her her rights! Wife, give him his rights!" (v. 3). And in verse 4, "Do not deprive one another."

Paul emphatically does not encourage the husband or wife who wants sexual gratification to seize it without concern for the other's needs. Instead he urges both husband and wife to always be ready to give their body when the other wants it.

I infer from this, and from Jesus's teaching in general, that happy and fulfilling sexual relations in marriage depend on each partner aiming to give satisfaction to the other. If it is the joy of each to make the other happy, a hundred problems will be solved.

Husbands, if it is your joy to bring her satisfaction, you will be sensitive to what she needs and wants. You will learn that the preparation for satisfactory sexual intercourse at 10 p.m. begins with tender words at 7 a.m. and continues through the day as kindness and respect. And when the time comes, you will not come on like a Sherman tank, but will know her pace and bring her skillfully along. Unless she gives you the signal, you will say, "Her climax, not mine, is the goal." And you will find in the long run that it is more blessed to give than to receive.

Wives, this is not always the case, but your husband may want sexual relations more often than you do. Martin Luther said he found twice a week to be ample protection from the tempter. I don't know if Katie, his wife, was up for it every time or not. But if you're not, give it anyway. I do not say to you husbands, "Take it anyway." In fact, for her sake you may go without. The goal is to outdo one another in giving what the other wants. Both of you, make it your aim to satisfy each other as fully as possible.

* * *

"Let marriage be held in honor among all, and let the marriage bed be undefiled." That is, do not sin in your sexual relations. And that means, have only those attitudes and do only those acts which come from faith in God's hope-giving promises. We should all regularly ask ourselves: "Does what I am feeling or doing have its roots in the contentment of faith or in the anxious insecurity of unbelief?" That will give you help in hundreds of little and big ethical decisions.

In this chapter, I have simply tried to show the impact of faith on three aspects of sexual relations in marriage.

First, faith believes God when he says that sexual relations in marriage are good and clean and should be received with thanksgiving by those who believe and know the truth.

Second, faith increases the joy of sexual relations in marriage because it frees from the guilt of the past. Faith believes the promise that Christ died for all our sins, that in him we might have guilt-free sexual relations in marriage.

And finally, faith wields the weapon of sexual intercourse against Satan. A married couple gives a severe blow to the head of that ancient serpent when they aim to give as much sexual satisfaction to each other as possible. It makes me just want to praise the Lord when I think that on top of all the joy that the sexual side of marriage brings, it also proves to be a fearsome weapon against our ancient foe.

But Hebrews 13 has much more to tell us about marriage. That's why we return to it in the following chapter.

HEBREWS 13:1-6

Let brotherly love continue. [2] Do not neglect to show hospitality to strangers, for thereby some have entertained angels unawares. [3] Remember those who are in prison, as though in prison with them, and those who are mistreated, since you also are in the body. [4] Let marriage be held in honor among all, and let the marriage bed be undefiled, for God will judge the sexually immoral and adulterous. [5] Keep your life free from love of money, and be content with what you have, for he has said, "I will never leave you nor forsake you." [6] So we can confidently say,

"The Lord is my helper;
I will not fear;
what can man do to me?"

5
Let Marriage Be Held in Honor among All

Following on from the previous chapter, let's reexamine Hebrews 13, starting with verse 4, this time emphasizing what it means for a Christian couple to *honor* marriage—especially their own—in public and in private.

Honoring Marriage as Precious

The first thing to know is that the word for *honor* in the New Testament more commonly means "precious." It's the word used in 1 Corinthians 3:12 where Paul speaks of "gold, silver, precious stones." It's used in 1 Peter 1:19 to reference the "precious blood" of Jesus. It's used in 2 Peter 1:4 to refer to the "precious and very great promises" of God.

So when Hebrews 13:4 says, "Let marriage be held in honor among all," we should hear the ring of preciousness. The Bible is telling us to let marriage—especially your own marriage—always be thought of as precious. Let it be treasured like gold and silver and rare jewels. Let it be revered and respected like the noblest, most virtuous person you have ever known. Let it be esteemed and valued as something terribly rare and costly. When you think of marriage—your marriage—let yourself be gripped by emotions of tremendous respect and sanctity. Cultivate the feeling that marriage is not to be touched quickly or handled casually or treated commonly. In God's eyes marriage is precious and therefore he says, "Let marriage be held in honor among all."

How to be Salty

My aim here is to call you, in the name of Jesus and for the glory of God and for the good of yourself and your community, to be in sync with God about your marriage, and out of sync with secular western culture.

One summer we were reading through Luke as a family, and one day we got to the end of chapter 14 where Jesus essentially says, "Whoever of you does not renounce all that he has cannot be my disciple." Jesus calls for a radical detachment from things—the things of this world—for the sake of the kingdom. Then, seemingly out of the blue, he says, "Salt is good, but if salt has lost its taste, how shall its saltiness be restored? It is of no use either for the soil or for the manure pile. It is thrown away. He who has ears to hear, let him hear" (Luke 14:34–35).

What's the connection? I suggested to the family (and now to you) that Christians are the salt of the earth to the degree that we are out of step with the values of the world and in step with the values of God. All the nations seek what to wear and eat and drink and drive and play with.

But you must be free of all that and seek the kingdom first, and then you will be salt.

The world is like a piece of cheap, tasteless hamburger. It's blah. It needs salt to preserve it and give it the spice of eternal joy. But so much of the church today is taking its cues from the world—online, on TV, on the radio and podcasts, in magazines and apps and newspapers—with voices that simply put a religious gloss on the language of secular culture, and it all just exposes the fact that much of the church is itself another piece of blah hamburger. And when that church lands on the world, you don't get a salty hamburger. All you get is two pieces of blah, unsalted, unappetizing, spiritually joyless hamburger.

So I am calling you to be out of step with the world on the matter of marriage. To get your cues for how to think and feel about your marriage not from the spirit of our age but from God, who made heaven and earth and everything in them—including marriage—for the glory of his name and the good of his people. That's how you become salty.

Tasting the Salt in Hebrews 13

Let's look at the context of Hebrews 13:4 to get the flavor of this command to honor marriage. It really is a salty context. This is not a blah list of rules for Christian behavior. It's a context of love and compassion and confidence and hope and freedom. It's salty.

- Verse 1 says, "Let brotherly love continue," so keep on loving Christians. Build a fellowship of deep affection for each other.

- Verse 2 tells us to not just love familiar Christians; love strangers too. Show them hospitality (discussed in Appendix 2). God will surprise you with unexpected blessings.
- Verse 3 says we should love prisoners and the ones who are being ill-treated.

So love fellow believers, love strangers, love prisoners. Then comes verse 4, about honoring marriage and keeping the marriage bed pure. As we saw in the previous chapter, this is followed by "Keep your life free from love of money," in verse 5. And this is followed by the liberating promises that God will never leave you or forsake you, but will be your helper, so you don't need to crave money if you trust God.

Now I think this is a salty paragraph. This is radical Jesus-kind-of-living. Don't love money. Trust God. Love Christians, love strangers, love prisoners, love the hurting. And right in the middle of all that radical, salty, non-world-like, God-like way of living, it says, "Let marriage be held in honor among all, and let the marriage bed be undefiled."

I don't know how you hear this command for your marriage. Here's how I hear it, and I hope you do too. When it comes right in the midst of love Christians, love strangers, love prisoners, love the hurting, don't love money, trust God to take care of you—when honoring marriage comes right in the middle of that kind of God-talk, I hear it as good news. Honoring marriage—especially your marriage—is like loving Christians. Honoring your marriage is like loving strangers. Honoring your marriage is like loving prisoners. Honoring your marriage is like not loving money because God wants to take care of you.

And so when I see at the end of verse 4, "God will judge the sexually immoral and adulterous"—that is, God will judge those who defile the marriage bed, those who dishonor marriage—when I hear that warning, I don't hear a trigger-happy God. I don't hear a quick-tempered God just waiting to zap a fornicator or an adulterer. What I hear is the sober, truthful reinforcement of *love for people*.

God loves it when we love Christians, and he loves it when we love strangers, and he loves it when we love prisoners, and he loves it when we don't love money but trust him for our needs, and he loves it when we honor marriage. Why? Because love is good for Christians, and love is good for strangers, and love is good for prisoners, and not loving money is good for our souls, and honoring marriage is good for us and for our society. And Therefore God would be unloving if he did not judge those who demean marriage and defile it and cheapen it and ridicule it and treat it with contempt.

I hope you taste the exciting flavor of Hebrews 13:1–6, because it is wonderfully salty. It has a lot of God in it and a lot of love and a big helping of ultimate issues like the warning of judgment and the promise that God will never leave us or forsake us if we trust him. When the Bible calls us to honor marriage, to keep the marriage bed pure, may we hear it as part of the overall call of Jesus to be radical, free, loving, salty, counter-cultural Christians.

Specific Ways to Hold Marriage in Honor

By way of application, let me offer some thoughts that may help you relate biblically to a morally disintegrating culture.

I will do this by drawing out some specific ways the two of you can hold marriage in honor, now and in the future.

1. Don't Confuse It with Anything That Is Not Marriage

What I have in mind here is a homosexual relationship between two men or two women. We live in tumultuous times. Up until the last few decades, as far as we know, no society in the history of the world had ever defined marriage as including between people of the same sex. It is a mind-boggling innovation with no precedent.

These thousands of years of unified human behavior are no fluke of history. The apostle Paul tells us that homosexual relations are revealed as sin not only in Christian Scripture, but in nature as well.

> God gave them up to dishonorable passions. For their women exchanged *natural* relations for those that are *contrary to nature*; and the men likewise gave up *natural* relations with women and were consumed with passion for one another, men committing shameless acts with men and receiving in themselves the due penalty for their error. (Romans 1:26–27)

This God-designed *naturalness* has been recognized, as far as we know, for the entire history of humankind, until the last few decades. This is why I say we live in tumultuous times. So as you are looking forward to marriage, let me try to show you briefly from Scripture why this precious institution is not and cannot be a union between two people of the same sex.

Marriage is created and defined by God in the Scriptures as *the sexual and covenantal union of a man and a woman in life-long allegiance to each other alone, as husband and wife, with a view to displaying Christ's covenant relationship to his blood-bought church.* Consider four passages of Scripture to support this definition.

Created Male and Female

> *God created man in his own image, in the image of God he created him; male and female he created them. And God blessed them. And God said to them, "Be fruitful and multiply and fill the earth"* |
> *(Genesis 1:27–28).*

So God created man as male and female with a mission of filling the earth with his glory—since they are created in the image of that glory, and exist to reflect the beauty and greatness of God in the world. Humanity, from the very beginning, was male and female—two different kinds of glorious human beings.

One-Flesh Covenantal Union

In the following chapter of Genesis, God linked his design for male and female with marriage. When the woman is created from Adam's side, he exclaims, "'This at last is bone of my bones and flesh of my flesh; she shall be called Woman, because she was taken out of Man.' Therefore, a man shall leave his father and his mother and hold fast to his wife, and they shall become one flesh" (Genesis 2:23–24).

God created man male and female so that there might be a "one flesh" sexual union and covenantal cleaving ("hold fast") with a view to multiplying the human race and displaying God's covenant with his people. We will see in a moment that designing marriage on the pattern of God's relationship to his people is a profound mystery that will not be fully revealed until Christ comes.

Design for Marriage

Jesus, picking up on this link between creation and marriage and life-long covenant, wove together these two texts.

> Have you not read that he who created them from the beginning made them male and female [Genesis 1:27], and said [quoting Genesis 2:24], "Therefore [linking creation and marriage] a man shall leave his father and his mother and hold fast to his wife, and the two shall become one flesh?" So they are no longer two but one flesh. What therefore God has joined together, let not man separate. (Matthew 19:4–6)

By weaving together the marriage passage with the creation of mankind as male and female, Jesus shows that the joining of maleness and femaleness *is an essential part of God's design for every marriage.* What has God "joined together" in marriage? One man, and one woman. Today, in our new era of sexual experimentation and aberration, this can be a highly controversial position.

Reflecting Christ and the Church

One more passage makes even more clear that maleness and femaleness are essential to the deepest meaning of marriage—the profound mystery that Paul refers to.

> Now as the church submits to Christ, so also wives should submit in everything to their

husbands. Husbands, love your wives, as Christ loved the church and gave himself up for her.... "Therefore [quoting Genesis 2:24] a man shall leave his father and mother and hold fast to his wife, and the two shall become one flesh." This mystery is profound, and I am saying that it refers to Christ and the church.

From the beginning there has been a mysterious and profound meaning to marriage, even beyond what was revealed in nature. Paul is now opening that mystery. And the mystery is this: God made man male and female with their distinctive feminine and masculine natures and their distinctive roles so that in marriage as husband and wife they could display the covenant love between Christ and the church.

Which means that the basic roles of wife and husband are not interchangeable. The husband displays the sacrificial love of Christ's headship, and the wife submits to that headship with joy and displays the covenant-keeping role that God designed for his people. The mystery of marriage is that God had this double display in mind (of church and Christ, wife and husband) when he created man as male and female. The profoundest reality in the universe underlies marriage as a covenantal union between a man and a woman.

Therefore, same-sex partnerships cannot embody what God designed marriage to be. Two men or two women cannot portray the mystery God designed for man and woman to display in marriage. Put simply and plainly, *there is no such thing as "same-sex marriage."* A government may decide to legalize it and call it marriage, but it is not.

So my point here is not only that so-called same-sex marriage *shouldn't* exist, but that it *doesn't* and it *can't*.

I don't want to leave you with the wrong impression here. Same-sex *inclinations* are not in the same category as same-sex practices. When the Bible says that "men who *practice* homosexuality" will not "inherit the kingdom of God" (1 Corinthians 6:10), it is referring to unrepentant rejection of God's truth and the practice of homosexual relations. Many godly men and women who experience same-sex attraction reject those inclinations as their defining reality and live lives of self-denial and sexual purity—just as thousands of single people do whose heterosexual desires are not acted on outside marriage.

As you move toward marriage, my prayer for you is that you will build your relationship on the gospel of Jesus Christ, which enables you to again and again forgive each other and rebuild gospel joy after sin has brought you into wounding conflict.

If you build your marriage on the gospel in this way, you will together have a gracious ministry to broken and sinful people outside your marriage. This includes a gracious demeanor and a welcoming home to those with same-sex attraction. You will live in the light not only of 1 Corinthians 6:10 (with its strong warning against homosexual practice), but you will also live in the hope-filled light of the next verse: "And such were some of you. But you were washed, you were sanctified, you were justified in the name of the Lord Jesus Christ and by the Spirit of our God"

This is the heart of biblical Christianity, in marriage and outside of marriage: "Such *were* some of you." There were Christians in the church at Corinth who *had been* fornicators and adulterers and thieves and drunkards and

"men who practice[d] homosexuality." When they turned
to Christ for hope and help in their battle with sin, they
were not driven away. They were folded in.

The way they were folded in was that they were
"justified in the name of the Lord Jesus Christ." That is,
they put their trust in Jesus; they turned from their sinful
practice; they renounced the sinful pursuit of their desires;
and God counted them righteous—he imputed to them
his own purity, and counted them as acceptable in his sight,
and adopted them into his family. Into our family.

May your marriage be this kind of gospel-saturated
marriage. May you stand firm and strong in our tumultuous
time in your commitment to marriage as *the sexual and covenantal union of a man and a woman in life-long allegiance to
each other alone, as husband and wife, with a view to displaying
the unbreakable covenant love between Christ and his church.*

This vision of marriage will bring the greatest blessing
you both, and make you a great blessing to others who
desperately need to see the beauty of the gospel lived out
in your marriage.

2. Don't Commit Fornication or Adultery

The second way to honor marriage is to not commit fornication or adultery.

That's what the second half of the verse says: "Let
the marriage bed be undefiled, for God will judge the
sexually immoral and adulterous." The word translated
"sexually immoral" means those who commit fornication
in distinction to adultery. The writer has two ways in mind
of dishonoring marriage and defiling the marriage bed:
adultery and fornication. Both at root commit the same
evil: having sexual relations with someone who is not your

lawful spouse. It's called adultery if you are married; it's called fornication if you are not married.

But both are a dishonor to marriage and a defiling of the marriage bed, because God made marriage, and marriage alone, as the one holy and safe and ultimately joyful place for sexual relations (cf. 1 Corinthians 7:2). The text says that God will judge fornicators and adulterers because they dishonor marriage and defile the marriage bed. In other words, God's judgment falls on unrepentant people who destroy what is meant for joy.

That word *repentant* leads to a third and final way to honor marriage and keep the marriage bed undefiled (though there are many more).

3. Live Out Forgiveness and Joy and Hope

We honor marriage when we live out the clean and happy future of our unclean and forgiven past.

The text tells us that God will judge fornicators and adulterers. First Corinthians 6:9 affirms this, then verse 11 says, "And such were some of you. But you were washed, you were sanctified, you were justified in the name of the Lord Jesus Christ and by the Spirit of our God."

Clearly there is judgment on fornicators and adulterers, but not all of them. There is escape from judgment for some. Hebrews teaches this message very clearly. In Hebrews 9:27–28 it says, "Just as it is appointed for man to die once, and after that comes judgment, so Christ, having been offered once to bear the sins of many, will appear a second time, not to deal with sin but to save those who are eagerly waiting for him."

So you can see there *will* be a judgment. But Christ has borne the sins of many—he has taken the judgment for their fornication and their adultery upon himself. And now he is coming, not to do that again, but to save us from the final judgment.

Or look at Hebrews 10:12–13, "But when Christ had offered for all time a single sacrifice for sins, he sat down at the right hand of God, waiting from that time until his enemies should be made a footstool for his feet." So again, you see two things: Christ took sins like fornication and adultery upon himself and paid their penalty in his own death. *But* there is coming a time when his enemies will be made a footstool for his feet. There is a judgment.

We see, therefore, two groups of people: those whose sins are covered and forgiven by Jesus (Hebrews 8:12; 10:17), and those whose sins will come down on their own heads in the judgment. The difference is in turning from sin and coming to God through Jesus for forgiveness and help. Hebrews 7:25 says that Jesus "is able to save to the uttermost those who draw near to God through him." So throughout your engagement and marriage, turn and continue turning from fornication. Turn and continue turning from adultery. Draw near to God through Jesus, and he will save for all time. He will enable you to live out a clean and happy future from an unclean and forgiven past.

Why This Kind of Living Honors Marriage

This living out of forgiveness and hope honors marriage, because God created marriage to be a living drama of the loving relationship between Christ and his bride, the church (again, see Ephesians 5). So the people who honor this intention best are the people who live out the very forgiveness and cleanness and joy that God designed marriage to portray.

There is so much more that could be said. So I leave the rest for the work of the Holy Spirit and the Word of God and prayer in your life. May God make you a salty couple—people whose lives portray good and do good for our decaying society.

6

The Surpassing Goal: Marriage Lived for the Glory of God

My topic for this closing chapter is, "Marriage lived for the glory of God," a natural follow-on to all that has come before in this book. The topic is not, "The glory of God *for* the living of marriage." And it is not, "Marriage lived *by* the glory of God." But it is, "Marriage lived for the glory of God."

This little word *for* means that there is an order of priority, of ultimacy. And the order is plain: God is ultimate, and marriage is not. God is the most important Reality; marriage is less important—far less important, infinitely less important.

Marriage exists to magnify the truth and worth and beauty and greatness of God; God does not exist to magnify marriage. Until this order is vivid and valued—until it is seen and savored—you will not experience marriage as a revelation of God's glory but as a rival of God's glory.

I take my topic, "Marriage lived for the glory of God,"

to be an answer to the question: *Why marriage?* Why is there marriage? Why does marriage exist? Why do we live in marriages?

This means that my topic is part of a larger question: Why does anything exist? Why do you exist? Why does sex exist? Why do earth and sun and moon and stars exist? Why do animals and plants and oceans and mountains and atoms and galaxies exist?

The answer to all these questions, including the one about marriage, is that all of them exist to and for the glory of God. That is, they exist to magnify the truth and worth and beauty and greatness of God. Not the way a *microscope* magnifies, but the way a *telescope* magnifies.

Microscopes magnify by making tiny things look bigger than they are. Telescopes magnify by making unimaginably big things look more like what they really are. Microscopes move the appearance of size away from reality. Telescopes move the appearance of size toward reality.

When I say that all things exist to magnify the truth and worth and beauty and greatness of God, I mean that all things—and marriage in particular—exist to move the appearance of God in people's minds toward Reality.

Ultimate Reality

God is unimaginably great and infinitely valuable and unsurpassed in beauty. "Great is the LORD, and greatly to be praised, and his greatness is unsearchable" (Psalm 145:3). Everything that exists is meant to magnify that Reality. God cries out through the prophet Isaiah, "Bring my sons from afar and my daughters from the end of the earth, everyone who is called by my name, whom I created *for my glory*" (Isaiah 43:6–7). We have been created to display the glory of God.

Paul concludes the first eleven chapters of his great letter to the Romans with the exaltation of God as the source and end of all things: "For from him and through him and to him are all things. To him be glory forever. Amen" (Romans 11:36). He makes it even clearer in Colossians 1:16, where he says, "By [Christ] all things were created, in heaven and on earth... all things were created through him and for him."

And woe to us if we think that *for him* means "for his need," or "for his benefit," or "for his improvement." Paul made it crystal clear in Acts 17:25 that God is not "served by human hands, as though he needed anything, since he himself gives to all mankind life and breath and everything." No, *for his glory* and *for him* mean "for the display of his glory," or "for the showing of his glory," or "for the magnifying of his glory."

We need to let this sink in. Once there was God, and only God. The universe is his creation. It is not coeternal with God. It is not God. "In the beginning was the Word, and the Word was with God, and the Word was God.... All things were made through him" (John 1:1, 3). All things. All that is not God was made by God. So at one time, there was only God.

Therefore, God is absolute Reality. We are not. The universe is not. Marriage is not. The human race is neither the ultimate reality, nor the ultimate value, nor the ultimate measuring rod of what is good or true or beautiful. God is. God is the one ultimate absolute in existence. Everything else is from him and through him and for him.

This is the starting place for understanding your marriage. Get this wrong, and everything goes wrong. Get it right—really right, in your heads and in your hearts—and your marriage will be transformed by it. Your marriage will become what it was created by God to be—a display of the truth and worth and beauty and greatness of God.

Less Marriage, More God

This leads to a very simple conclusion, so simple and yet so far-reaching. If we who are believers in Jesus want to see marriage have the place in the world and in the church that it is supposed to have—that is, if we want marriage to glorify the truth and worth and beauty and greatness of God—we must teach and preach less about marriage and more about God.

Most young people today, it must be said, do not bring to their courtship and marriage a great vision of God— who he is, what he is like, how he acts. In the world there is almost no vision of God. He is not even on the list to be invited. He is simply and breathtakingly omitted. And in the church, the view of God that young couples bring to their relationship is so often small instead of huge—and so often marginal instead of central, and so often vague instead of clear, and so often impotent instead of all-determining, and so often uninspiring instead of ravishing—that when they marry, the thought of living marriage to the glory of God is without meaning and without content.

What would the glory of God mean to a young wife or husband who gives almost no time and no thought to *knowing* the glory of God, or the glory of Jesus Christ, his divine Son...

> the glory of his eternality that makes the mind want to explode with the infinite thought that God never had a beginning, but simply always was;

> the glory of his knowledge that makes the Library of Congress look like a matchbox, and quantum physics like a first-grade reader;

> the glory of his wisdom that has never been and can never be counseled by men;

> the glory of his authority over heaven and earth and hell, without whose permission no man and no demon can move one inch;

> the glory of his providence, without which not one bird falls to the ground or a single hair turns gray;

> the glory of his word that upholds the universe and keeps all the atoms and molecules together;

> the glory of his power to walk on water, cleanse lepers, heal the lame, open the eyes of the blind, cause the deaf to hear, still storms with a word, and raise the dead;

> the glory of his purity never to sin, or to have a two-second bad attitude or evil thought;

> the glory of his trustworthiness never to break his word or let one promise fall to the ground;

> the glory of his justice to render all moral accounts in the universe settled, either on the cross or in hell;

> the glory of his patience to endure our dullness for decade after decade;

> the glory of his sovereign, slave-like obedience to embrace the excruciating pain of the cross willingly;

> the glory of his wrath that will one day cause people to call out for the rocks and the mountains to fall on them;

> ‣ the glory of his grace that justifies the ungodly; and
> ‣ the glory of his love that dies for us even while we were sinners.

How could people even begin to live their lives so that their marriages display the truth and worth and beauty and greatness of this glory, when they devote almost no energy or time to knowing and cherishing this glory?

Perhaps you can understand why I have come to see my life-mission in very basic terms: to spread a passion for the supremacy of God in all things for the joy of all peoples. That's the need. Until there is a passion for the supremacy and the glory of God in the hearts of married people, marriage will not be lived for the glory of God.

And there will not be a passion for the supremacy and the glory of God in the hearts of married people until God himself, in his manifold glories, is known. And he will not be known in his manifold glories until pastors and teachers speak of him tirelessly and constantly and deeply and biblically and faithfully and distinctly and thoroughly and passionately. Marriage lived for the glory of God will be the fruit of churches permeated with the glory of God.

So I say again, if believers in Jesus want marriage to glorify the truth and worth and beauty and greatness of God, we must teach and preach less about marriage and more about God. Not that we preach too much on marriage, but that we preach too little on God. God is simply not magnificently central in the lives of most Christians. He is not the sun around which all the planets of our daily lives are held in orbit and find their proper, God-appointed place. He is more like the moon, which waxes and wanes, and you can go for nights and never think about it.

For most believers God is marginal, and a hundred good but secondary things usurp his place. To think that marriages could be lived for his glory by teaching on the dynamics of relationships, when the glory of God is so peripheral, is like expecting the human eye to glorify the stars when we don't stare at the night sky and have never bought a telescope.

Unlock a Thousand Doors

Knowing God and cherishing God and valuing the glory of God above all things, including your spouse, will be the key to living your marriage to the glory of God. It's true in marriage, as in every other relationship: God is most glorified in us when we are most satisfied in him.

Here is a key that unlocks a thousand doors. Superior satisfaction in God above all earthly things, including your spouse and your health and your own life (Psalm 63:3, "your steadfast love is better than life") is the source of great long-suffering—without which husbands cannot love like Christ and wives cannot follow like the bride of Christ, the church. Ephesians 5:22–25 makes plain that husbands need to take their cues of leadership and love from Christ, and wives need to take their cues of submission and love from the Godward devotion of the church for whom he died. And both of those complementary acts of love—to lead, and to submit—are unsustainable for the glory of God without a superior satisfaction in all that God is for us in Christ.

Let me say it another way. There are two levels at which the glory of God may shine forth from your marriage. One is at the structural level, when both you and your spouse fulfill the roles God intended—the man as a leader like Christ, the wife as an advocate and follower of that leadership. When those roles are lived out, the glory of God's love and wisdom in Christ is displayed to the world.

But there is another, deeper, more foundational level where the glory of God must shine if these roles are to be sustained in your marriage as God designed them. The power and impulse to carry through the self-denial and the daily, monthly, yearly dying that will be required in order to love an imperfect wife and respect an imperfect husband must come from a hope-giving, soul-sustaining, superior satisfaction in God. I don't think that the mutual love of spouses for one another can glorify God at this level until it flows from a heart that delights in God *more than in marriage*.

Your marriage will be preserved for the glory of God and shaped for the glory of God when the glory of God is more precious to you than is your marriage. When you can say with the apostle Paul, "I count all things to be loss in view of the surpassing value of knowing Christ Jesus my Lord" (Philippians 3:8, NASB). When you can say *that* about *your* marriage, about your husband or wife, then your marriage will be lived to the glory of God.

I close by trying to say this one more way, namely, with a poem that I wrote for my son on his wedding day.

LOVE HER MORE AND LOVE HER LESS

For Karsten Luke Piper at His Wedding to Rochelle Ann Orvis
May 29, 1995

The God whom we have loved, and in
Whom we have lived, and who has been
Our Rock these twenty-two good years
With you, now bids us, with sweet tears,
To let you go: "A man shall leave
His father and his mother, cleave
Henceforth unto his wife, and be
One unashaméd flesh and free."
This is the word of God today,
And we are happy to obey.
For God has given you a bride
Who answers every prayer we've cried
For over twenty years, our claim
For you, before we knew her name.

And now you ask that I should write
A poem—a risky thing, in light
Of what you know: that I am more
The preacher than the poet or
The artist. I am honored by
Your bravery, and I comply.
I do not grudge these sweet confines
Of rhyming pairs and metered lines.
They are old friends.
They like it when

I bid them help me once again
To gather feelings into form
And keep them durable and warm.

And so we met in recent days,
And made the flood of love and praise
And counsel from a father's heart
To flow within the banks of art.
Here is a portion of the stream,
My son: a sermon poem. Its theme:
A double rule of love that shocks;
A doctrine in a paradox:

If you now aim your wife to bless,
Then love her more and love her less.

If in the coming years, by some
Strange providence of God, you come
To have the riches of this age,
And, painless, stride across the stage
Beside your wife, be sure in health
To love her, love her more than wealth.

And if your life is woven in
A hundred friendships, and you spin
A festal fabric out of all
Your sweet affections, great and small,
Be sure, no matter how it rends,
To love her, love her more than friends.

And if there comes a point when you
Are tired, and pity whispers, "Do

Yourself a favor. Come, be free;
Embrace the comforts here with me."
Know this! Your wife surpasses these:
So love her, love her more than ease.

And when your marriage bed is pure,
And there is not the slightest lure
Of lust for any but your wife,
And all is ecstasy in life,
A secret all of this protects:
Go love her, love her more than sex.

And if your taste becomes refined,
And you are moved by what the mind
Of man can make, and dazzled by
His craft, remember that the "why"
Of all this work is in the heart;
So love her, love her more than art.

And if your own should someday be
The craft that critics all agree
Is worthy of a great esteem,
And sales exceed your wildest dream,
Beware the dangers of a name.
And love her, love her more than fame.

And if, to your surprise, not mine,
God calls you by some strange design
To risk your life for some great cause,
Let neither fear nor love give pause,
And when you face the gate of death,
Then love her, love her more than breath.

Yes, love her, love her, more than life;
Oh, love the woman called your wife.
Go love her as your earthly best.
Beyond this venture not. But, lest
Your love become a fool's facade,
Be sure to love her less than God.

It is not wise or kind to call
An idol by sweet names, and fall,
As in humility, before
A likeness of your God.
Adore Above your best beloved on earth
The God alone who gives her worth.
And she will know in second place
That your great love is also grace,
And that your high affections now
Are flowing freely from a vow
Beneath these promises, first made
To you by God. Nor will they fade
For being rooted by the stream
Of Heaven's Joy, which you esteem
And cherish more than breath and life,
That you may give it to your wife.

The greatest gift you give your wife
Is loving God above her life.
And thus I bid you now to bless:
Go love her more by loving less.

APPENDIX 1

Some Questions to Ask When Preparing for Marriage

Theology

▸ What do you believe about...everything? To get started, perhaps read through the Desiring God Affirmation of Faith to see where each other is on various biblical doctrines (www.desiringgod.org/affirmation-of-faith).

▸ Discover how you form your views. What is your "reasoning-believing process"? How do you handle the Bible?

Worship and Devotions

▸ How important is corporate worship and local-church membership? What about other kinds of participations in church life? What does it mean to be active in a local church?

- How important is it to be part of a small accountability/support group?
- What is the importance of music in life and worship?
- What are your daily personal devotional practices? (prayer, reading, meditation, memorization)
- What would our family devotions look like? Who would lead in this?
- Are we doing this now in an appropriate way (praying together about our lives and future, reading the Bible together)?

Husband and Wife

- What is the meaning of headship and submission in the Bible and in our marriage?
- What expectations should we have about situations where one of us might be alone with someone of the opposite sex?
- How will we share tasks in the home (finances, cleaning, cooking, washing dishes, yard work, car upkeep, repairs, shopping for food, other household stuff)?
- What are our expectations for togetherness?
- What is an ideal non-special evening?
- How do we understand who initiates sex and how often?
- Who does the checkbook—or are there two?

Children

- If and when should we have children? Why?
- How many?
- How far apart?
- Would we consider adoption?

- What are our expectations for our children's' standards of behavior? Can these differ from one child to another and still be biblical?
- How do we distinguish between punishment and discipline?
- What are appropriate ways to discipline young children physically? How many strikes before they're... whatever? Up to what age? What other forms of discipline can be appropriate?
- What are our expectations of time spent with our children? Bedtime rituals?
- What signs of affection will we show them?
- What about school? Home school? Christian school? Public school?

Lifestyle

- Own a home or not? Why?
- What kind of neighborhood? Why?
- How many cars? New? Used?
- What kind of vacations will be appropriate and helpful for us?
- View of money in general? How much to the church?
- How will we spend our weekends and "time off"?
- How do you make money decisions?
- What about buying clothes? New? Thrift store? In between? Designer label? Current fashions? Why?

Entertainment

- How much should we spend on entertainment?
- How often should we eat out? Where?

- How about grown-up toys? Recreational vehicles? Computer gaming? Sports equipment? Hobby gear?
- Should we have a television? Where? What is fitting to watch? How much?
- What are our criteria for movies and theater? What will our guidelines be for the kids?

Conflict

- What makes you angry?
- How do you handle your frustration or anger?
- Who should bring up an issue that is bothersome?
- What if we disagree both about what should be done and whether it is serious?
- Will we go to bed angry at each other?
- What is our view of getting help from friends or counselors?

Work

- Who will be the main breadwinner?
- Should the wife work outside the home? Before kids? With kids at home? After kids?
- What are our views of daycare for children?
- What determines where we will locate? Job? Whose job? Church? Family?

Friends

- Is it sometimes good to do things with friends but without your spouse?
- What will we do if one of us really likes to hang out with someone the other doesn't?

Health and Sickness

- Do you have, or have you had, any sicknesses or other problems that could affect our relationship? (allergies, cancer, eating disorders, venereal disease, depression, frequent illness, pain issues, etc.)
- Do you believe in divine healing, and how would prayer relate to medical attention?
- How do you think about exercise and healthy eating?
- Do you have any habits that adversely affect your health?

Differences

- How do you handle and live with differences between people?
- How do you decide what can remain differences without jeopardizing the relationship?

1 PETER 4:7-11

The end of all things is at hand; therefore be self-controlled and sober-minded for the sake of your prayers. [8] Above all, keep loving one another earnestly, since love covers a multitude of sins. [9] Show hospitality to one another without grumbling. [10] As each has received a gift, use it to serve one another, as good stewards of God's varied grace: [11] whoever speaks, as one who speaks oracles of God; whoever serves, as one who serves by the strength that God supplies—in order that in everything God may be glorified through Jesus Christ. To him belong glory and dominion forever and ever. Amen.

The Christian Virtue of Hospitality

A Christ-Exalting Strategy of Love in the Last Days

What's driving this final appendix is a desire for Christ to be magnified in the way married people (and single people, for that matter) show hospitality to each other. After all, is God's family—come into being by new birth and faith in Christ—is that family more central and more lasting than natural families which come into being by marriage and procreation and adoption? I believe it is, and that therefore how the members of that spiritual, eternal family (the church) relate to each other (married and single) is a crucial witness to the world—a witness that our lives are oriented on the supremacy of Christ and our relationships are defined not just by nature, but by Christ. I long to see Christ magnified through married people folding single people into their lives, and single people folding married people into their lives, for the sake of Christ and the gospel.

Jesus said, "Whoever gives one of these little ones

even a cup of cold water because he is a disciple, truly, I
say to you, he will by no means lose his reward" (Matthew
10:42). Of course, Jesus also said that we should love our
enemy (Matthew 5:44), and Paul said to give a cup of
water to our enemy (Romans 12:20). That kind of love will
receive its reward. But here Jesus essentially says that we
should show simple kindness to people precisely because
they are followers of Jesus. And that too will receive its
reward.

In other words, when in your marriage you look
into the eyes of someone and see the face of a follower of
Jesus—a brother or a sister of your own eternal family—
that shared relationship with Jesus should tend to draw
out your heart in practical kindness, such as hospitality, for
Jesus' sake. Jesus is the focus here. He says we are to do
this "because he is my disciple." Christ will be honored in
a special way if you give his disciple a drink *for that reason.*
"If you have him into your home," Jesus is telling us, "do
this for my sake."

The Material World for the Glory of God

We addressed this point generally a little earlier in this
book, but have you ever wondered, *Why did God give us
bodies and make a material universe?* It's a good and important question. Why does he raise our bodies from the
dead and make them new, and why will he, at his second
coming, then liberate this earth so that it is a new earth
that we can live on, forever, in our new bodies? If God
meant to have great praise ("Great is the LORD, and greatly
to be praised," Psalm 96:4), why not just create angels with

no bodies but great hearts who can speak only to God and not to each other? Why all these human bodies and why should persons be able to communicate with each other? And why trees and ground and water and fire and wind and lions and lambs and lilies and birds and bread and wine?

There are several deep and wonderful answers to these questions. But the one I want to mention is this: God made bodies and material things—and he made marriage—because when they are rightly seen and rightly used, God's glory is more fully known and displayed.

- "The heavens declare the glory of God" (Psalm 19:1).
- Consider the birds of the air and the lilies of the field and you will know more of God's goodness and care (see Matthew 6:26–28).
- See in the things he has made his "invisible attributes"—his "eternal power and divine nature" (Romans 1:20).
- Look at marriage and see Christ and the church (see Ephesians 5:23–25).
- "As often as you eat this bread and drink the cup, you proclaim the Lord's death until he comes" (1 Corinthians 11:26).
- "Whether you eat or drink, or whatever you do, do all to the glory of God" (1 Corinthians 10:31).

The material world within which your marriage will play out is not an end in itself; it is designed to display God's glory and awaken our hearts to know him and value him more.

Making Food and Sex Holy

Physical reality is good. God made it as a revelation of his glory. And he intends for us to sanctify it and worship him with it—that is, to see it in relation to him and to use it in a way that makes much of him and in doing so gives us joy. All of this has direct bearing on marriage and singleness. It protects us from idolizing sex and food as gods. They are not gods; they are made by God to honor God. And it protects us from fearing sex and food as evil. They are not evil; they are instruments of worship—they are ways to make much of Christ. The key text here is 1 Timothy 4:1–5. It is one of the most important texts in the Bible on the meaning of physical appetites or sex.

> Now the Spirit expressly says that in later times some will depart from the faith by devoting themselves to deceitful spirits and teachings of demons, through the insincerity of liars whose consciences are seared, who forbid marriage and require abstinence from foods that God created to be received with thanksgiving by those who believe and know the truth. For everything created by God is good, and nothing is to be rejected if it is received with thanksgiving, for it is made holy by the word of God and prayer.

Sex and food—two great idols in first-century Asia Minor and twenty-first-century America. And what is God's response to those who "solve" the problem of the idolatry of sex and food by merely renouncing or avoiding these things? He says these teachers are deceitful and demonic. God's solution is different. Everything he created is good;

nothing is to be rejected if it is received with thanksgiving and made holy by the word of God and prayer. You make food holy by using it according to the word of God in Christ-dependent prayer. And you make sex holy by using it according to the word of God in Christ-dependent prayer.

Making Much of Christ, Whether Single or Married

All of that is simply to say that neither marriage nor singleness are to be either idolized or feared. Not the beauty of marriage as a physical parable of the covenant love between Christ and the church. And not the beauty of singleness as a physical parable of the spiritual nature of God's family, the family that grows, not by sex and procreation, but by regeneration and faith.

Marriage *and* celibacy can be equally idolatrous. Spouses can worship each other or worship sex or worship their children or worship double-income, no-kid buying power. Singles can worship autonomy and independence. Singles can look on marriage as a second-class Christian compromise with one's sexual drive. Married people can look upon singleness as a mark of immaturity or irresponsibility or incompetence or even homosexuality.

What I am trying to clarify is that there are Christ-exalting ways to be married and there are Christ-exalting ways to be single. There are ways to use our bodies, our physical appetites, in marriage and in singleness, that make much of Christ.

And one last comment before we get to our 1 Peter text. It's about that infamous sentence in 1 Corinthians 7:9:

"If they cannot exercise self-control, they should marry. For it is better to marry than to burn with passion." Remember, in verse 8 this is addressed explicitly and equally to men and women. And here is the thing I want to emphasize about it: when a person seeks to be married, knowing that otherwise as a single he or she would "burn with passion," should that person in any way see this verse as indicating that marriage is primarily intended to serve as a mere channel for the sex drive? Certainly not. Paul would never mean that in view of the overall intent of Ephesians chapter 5.

Instead, when a person marries—and let me simply use the man as an example—he takes his sexual desire, and he does the same thing with it that we must *all* do with all our physical desires if we would make them means of worship:

1. he brings it into conformity to God's word;
2. he subordinates it to a higher pattern of love and care;
3. he transposes the music of physical pleasure into the music of spiritual worship;
4. he listens for the echoes of God's goodness in every nerve;
5. he seeks to double his pleasure by making her joy his joy; and
6. he gives thanks to God from the bottom of his heart because he knows and he feels that he never deserved one minute of this pleasure.

Magnifying Christ by Showing Hospitality

Now to 1 Peter 4:7–11, and what's driving this appendix, namely, a desire for Christ to be magnified in the way married people and single people show hospitality to each other. We will walk through the text quickly with brief comments, and then draw out simple and obvious implications, praying that God would use this word powerfully to change us for his glory and our joy.

The End Is Near

"The end of all things is at hand" (v. 7). Peter knows that with the coming of the Messiah the end of the ages has arrived (1 Corinthians 10:11; Hebrews 12:2). The kingdom of God has come (Luke 17:21). And therefore the consummation of all things could sweep over the world in a very short time.

So, just as Jesus taught us to be vigilant over our lives and to watch, Peter says, "Therefore be self-controlled and sober-minded for the sake of your prayers" (v. 7). That is, cultivate a very personal relationship with the one you hope to see face to face at his coming. Don't be unfamiliar with Christ. You don't want to meet him as a stranger. And seek in prayer all the help you will need in these last days so that you may stand in the days of great stress (see Luke 21:36). And don't depend on your spontaneity to bring you to prayer. "Be self-controlled and sober-minded for the sake of your prayers."

Love Is Paramount

Then verse 8: "Above all, keep loving one another earnestly, since love covers a multitude of sins." Love is paramount, and it will be needed all the more as the end draws near. Why? Because the pressures and stresses and tribulations of the last days will put relationships under tremendous stress.

But in these days we will need each other, and the world will be watching to see if we are real: "By this all people will know that you are my disciples, if you have love for one another" (John 13:35). Will we cover and bear and endure each other's faults and foibles, or will anger rule our hearts?

Hospitality without Grumbling

Verse 9 gives one form of that love, and is it telling that he mentions doing it without grumbling? "Show hospitality to one another without grumbling." If we are loving earnestly and love is covering a multitude of sins, then we will not grumble so easily, will we? Love covers much of what makes us grumble. So hospitality without grumbling is the calling of Christians in the last days. In the very days when your stress is high, and when there are sins that need covering, and when reasons to grumble abound—in those very days, Peter says, what we need to do is practice hospitality.

Our homes need to be open. Because our hearts are open. And our hearts are open because God's heart is open to us. Do you recall how John the apostle connected the love of God with our love for each other in relation to hospitality? He wrote in 1 John 3:16–17, "By this we know love, that [Jesus] laid down his life for us, and we ought to lay down our lives for the brothers. But if anyone has the world's goods and sees his brother in need, yet closes his heart against him, how does God's love abide in him?"

Stewards of God's Varied Grace

Finally, I will simply point out what happens when we get together in our homes. "As each has received a gift, use it to serve one another, as good stewards of God's varied grace" (v. 10). I love that phrase, "stewards of God's varied grace"! Every Christian is a steward—a custodian, a manager, a warden, a distributor, a servant—of God's varied grace. What a great reason to be alive! Every Christian lives on grace. "God is able to make all *grace* abound to you, so that having all sufficiency in all things at all times, you may abound in every good work" (2 Corinthians 9:8). If you are afraid of hospitality—that you don't have much personal strength or personal wealth—good. Then you won't intimidate anybody. You will depend all the more on God's grace. You will look all the more to the work of Christ and not your own work. And oh what a blessing people will receive.

Welcome One Another as Christ Has Welcomed You

So there it is: the Christian virtue of hospitality—a Christ-exalting strategy of love in the last days. If you belong to Christ, if you have by faith received his saving hospitality, which he paid for with his own blood, then extend this hospitality to others. "Welcome one another as Christ has welcomed you, for the glory of God" (Romans 15:7). You live on free grace every day. Be a good steward of it in hospitality.

And in your marriage, plan that your hospitality include both married and single people at various times—small groups, Sunday dinners, picnics, holiday celebrations. Don't make a big deal out of it. Just be natural. And don't forget that fellow believers come in all ages: eighty-year-olds and sixty-year-olds and fifty- and forty- and thirty- and twenty-year-olds, male and female, formerly married and never married, divorced and widowed. Think like a Christian. This is your family, more deeply and more eternally than your kinfolk.

I pray that the Lord would do this beautiful work among us—all of us. The end of all things is at hand. Let us be sober for our prayers. Let us love each other. Let us be good stewards of the varied grace of God, and let us show hospitality without grumbling. "Welcome one another as Christ has welcomed you."

---

desiringGod

Everyone wants to be happy. Our website was born and built for happiness. We want people everywhere to understand and embrace the truth that God is most glorified in us when we are most satisfied in him. We've collected more than thirty years of John Piper's speaking and writing, including translations into more than forty languages. We also provide a daily stream of new written, audio, and video resources to help you find truth, purpose, and satisfaction that never end. And it's all available free of charge, thanks to the generosity of people who've been blessed by the ministry.

If you want more resources for true happiness, or if you want to learn more about our work at Desiring God, we invite you to visit us at www.desiringGod.org.

Made in the USA
San Bernardino, CA
26 May 2018